To my grandson
Christian,
Forever my
friend.

For TucaChoo the toucan, a train engineer,

it's a special day - his birthday is here.

Blowing his whistle, no one he'd forget,

a visit with friends his train would go get.

First through a mountain TucaChoo's train would go. A dark tunnel to enter, the train light will glow. When he pulled on the chain the whistle blew, that wonderful train noise "choo-choo-choo-choo".

Chopped trees on a train brought down from a hill, cut into lumber at the sawmill. More trees are planted, now they are small, in many years they will grow tall.

SawZee the bear lives at the sawmill,

with a piece of wood he uses his skills.

A train whistle he carved the sound

was just right, TucaChoo thanked him

with delight.

You can travel by bus or travel by car. If you want to go fast you wouldn't get far. To get there from here across any terrain, the fastest way to go would be on a train.

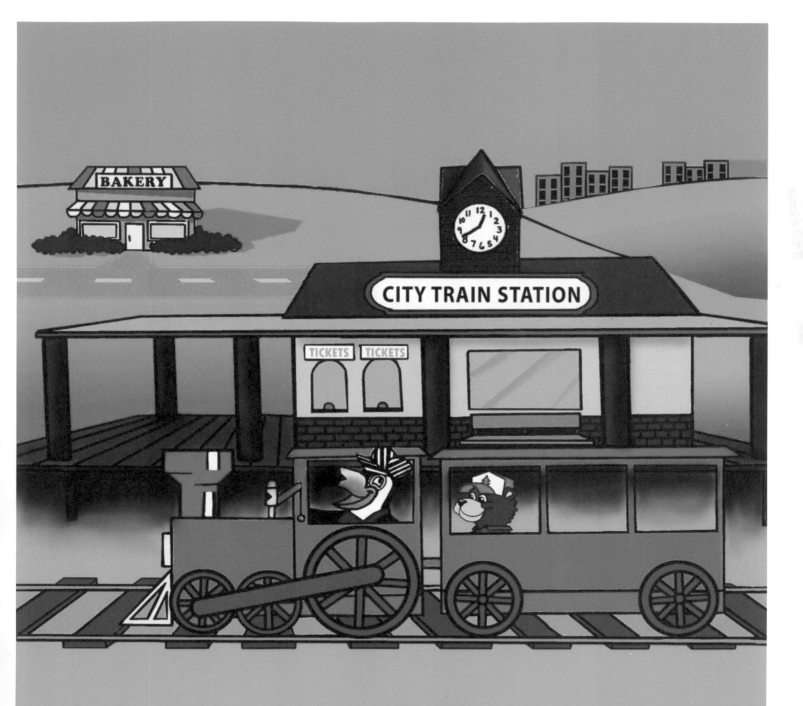

Into the city TucaChoo's train did stop,

behind the train station a bakery shop.

City Kitten was waiting and hiding a treat,

a cupcake she baked for TucaChoo to eat.

Three on the train and three more to go,

a bridge they would cross with water below.

Above the sky was periwinkle blue, yellow

and orange flowers below they grew.

Under the bridge lives Bridgett the duck,

a basket of flowers she did pluck.

A gift she needed for the birthday boy.

TucaChoo's friendship brought her

so much joy.

A visit to the dock was next on his trip,

boxes piled high on the cargo ship.

Moved by a crane so very slow,

onto a train boxes would go.

Seamore a shiprat in a sailor suit with blue stripes and red tie, he looked so cute. A beautiful seashell he found on the shore, a gift for TucaChoo not found in a store.

Grain in the silo filled to the top,

tied up in bales a yellow hay crop.

Brought to the feed store by train,

bales of hay and sacks of grain.

Haywood the farmer is one clever fox,

making a gift not bought in a box.

Weaved with hay for a big soft seat,

stuffed with grain a pillow complete.

Hugging each other TucaChoo had no

doubts, he looked at his friends

and out come a shout.

"Thank you for my gifts, I like them I do,

but the perfect gift I have is each of you".

CPSIA information can be obtained
at www.ICGtesting.com
Printed in the USA
LVHW072126240119
605217LV00017B/565/P